EARTH'S BIOMES

FOREST

EARTH'S BIOMES

FOREST

TOM WARHOL

Marshall Cavendish
Benchmark
New York

This book is dedicated to Bill Patterson for his unflagging faith and support.

Marshall Cavendish Benchmark
99 White Plains Road
Tarrytown, New York 10591-9001
www.marshallcavendish.us

Editor: Karen Ang
Editorial Director: Michelle Bisson
Art Director: Anahid Hamparian
Series Designer: Patrice Sheridan

Library of Congress Cataloging-in-Publication Data

Warhol, Tom.
Forest / by Tom Warhol.
p. cm. — (Earth's biomes)
Summary: "Explores forest biomes and covers where they are located as well
as the plants and animals that inhabit them" — Provided by publisher.
Includes bibliographical references and index.
ISBN-13: 978-0-7614-2189-4
ISBN-10: 0-7614-2189-0
1. Forests and forestry — Juvenile literature. 2. Forest ecology — Juvenile
literature. I. Title. II. Series.

QH86.W367 2007
577.3 — dc22
2006015821

Front cover: A rainforest in Borneo
Title page: A coniferous forest in Alaska
Back cover: A redwood forest

Photo research by Candlepants, Inc.

Cover Photo: Frans Lanting / Minden Pictures
The photographs in this book are used by permission and through the courtesy of:
Photo Researchers Inc.: Stephen J. Krasemann, 7; Susan McCartney, 12; Jim Zipp, 19; S.E. Cornelius, 23; Eye of
Science, 24; Gregory K. Scott, 31; Michael P. Gadomski, 48; Kenneth M. Highfill, 49; Alvin E. Staffan, 55; Art
Wolfe, 56; B.G. Thomson, 66. *Peter Arnold Inc:* BIOS, 8, 38; Steve Kaufman, 36; Ed Reschke, 37; Tapani
Rasanen/WWI, 42; Nick Bergkessel/UNEP, 52; Mark Edwards, 73. *Corbis:* Darell Gulin, 14; Charles Krebs, 44;
W.Cody, 46; Darrell Gulin, back cover. *Minden Pictures:* Ingo Arndt, 16; 22, ; Michael & Patricia Fogden, 22, 25,
64, 69; Dietmar Fullnill, 39; Michio Hoshino, 40; Pete Oxford, 58; Claus Meyer, 61; Frans Lanting, 63, 72; Konrad
Wothe, 67; Cyril Ruoso/JH Editorial, 70; SA Team/Foto Natura, 71. *Visuals Unlimited:* Inga Spence, 17. *Hans
Steur:* 26. *Tom Warhol:* 32, 47, 53. 2006 © *Gunther Matschke/Alaska Stock Photos:* 35.

Printed in China
1 3 5 6 4 2

CONTENTS

INTRODUCTION

FORESTS OF PLENTY

The wind rushes through the woods, carrying scents of decay and drying leaves—mint and wintergreen or the pungent aroma of pine resin. The bed of dry leaves on the ground rustles then floats into the air, forming a temporary mini-tornado that scatters across the forest floor as the wind passes. Tall trees bend back and forth, creaking and groaning like the squeaky hinge on a barn door. The treetops applaud softly and whisper the collective language of millions of leaves, punctuated by the clattering of branches. Suddenly, there's a loud crack, silence, and then a thud as a branch snaps off a tall tree and drops to the ground.

Within a few years, this branch will play host to a whole community of organisms—spores from nearby mushrooms will settle in the cracks and grooves, beginning the process of decay. Bacteria and other microbes will aid this process, and lichens and mosses will take advantage of the moisture and rich nutrients the decaying wood provides. Eventually, seeds from herbs and woody plants will find a spot, taking their share of the nutrients. Insects like beetles and carpenter ants will bore into the rotting wood, laying their eggs. Other moisture-loving bugs and salamanders will burrow into the rich, wet soil beneath the fallen log. These creatures will become food for voles, moles, mice,

A white-tailed deer buck pauses beneath oak trees.

birds, and other woodland creatures, who will then nourish carnivores like foxes, raccoons, chimpanzees, and the tamandua, an anteater from the South American rainforest. These small carnivores will then be preyed upon by larger meat-eaters like ocelots, wolves, and mountain lions. Humans will make use of some or all these species, from the trees to the mushrooms to the large animals, for shelter, fire, food, and clothing.

This general picture could fit many different forests in the world. These varied ecological communities make up what are known as forest biomes, complex biological communities dominated by trees and other woody plants. There are three major forest biomes in the world: boreal forest, temperate forest, and tropical forest. This doesn't mean there are only three kinds of forests, though. Within each of these biomes are many different forest types in many different stages of development.

Giant pandas live in the temperate forests of China, eating mostly bamboo.

1

FOREST FACTS

Most people in the world are familiar with forests. Forests grow everywhere that it is not too cold, too wet, or too dry. Near these extremes, plant life may still exist in a herbaceous (non-woody) form. But there's a level of dryness, wetness, and cold where no plant life exists. The greatest diversity, or variety of different life-forms, is at the equator in the tropical rainforests. This diversity decreases farther from the equator and higher in elevation. So, the areas with the least diversity are at the poles and on top of high mountains.

Scientists estimate that 50 percent, or 16 billion acres (almost 6.5 billion hectares), of Earth's land area was covered by forests 8,000 years ago. The Food and Agriculture Organization (FAO), a branch of the United Nations, determined in their Global Forest Resource Assessment that in 2000 the world's forests covered about 9.6 billion acres (3.9 billion ha). So Earth has lost 40 percent of its forest acres in only 8,000 years. That equals 6.4 billion acres (2.6 billion ha)—more than the total land area of North America and Central America combined. These natural forests have been replaced by other types of forests and plant communities or converted to farms, towns, or cities.

This table shows how the FAO broke down the different forests in the different regions of the world:

Region	Acres of forest	percent of world's land area	percent of world's forests
Europe	2,567,369,000	46	27
South America	2,189,306,000	51	23
Africa	1,606,150,000	22	17
Asia	1,354,108,000	18	14
North America and Central America	1,356,579,000	26	14
Oceania*	489,258,000	23	5

*including Australia, New Zealand, Papua New Guinea, and the Pacific Islands

Many of humankind's myths about forests tell of a dark and dangerous place where monsters hide, waiting for innocent humans to wander in. This belief comes from a fear of the unknown. As scientists learn more and more about rich and mysterious forest communities, we can learn to shed our fear and replace it with wonder and respect.

NATURAL RESOURCES

Forests are not simply a *part* of the world, they are primarily responsible for the clean air we breathe and the clean water we drink. Without the large and diverse assemblage of the world's plants, humans and all other life would cease to exist.

Most of the world's human population lives in or near forests. That's because they provide many things that humans need. The natural resources of the forest are plentiful.

Plants gathered by early explorers in the tropical forests, such as peppers and tomatoes, have become staples of the human diet. Jute, bamboo, and rattan—all from plants grown in forests—provide materials for many uses, including furniture-making. Resins from tropical trees provide base material for tires, chewing gum, inks, insecticides, soaps, and cosmetics. Many houseplants were first collected from tropical forests. Twenty-five percent of prescription drugs are made from tropical forest plants. Malaria, the tropical disease that kills more people than any other communicable disease (a disease passed from person to person), can be cured with quinine, a product of the tropical cinchona tree.

Wood from trees, one of the most obvious and important forest products, has provided warmth in the form of fire and building materials for shelter since early in human history. Paper is another important wood product. From books to paper towels, humans use an astonishing amount of paper every day. The boreal and temperate forests have long provided for the bulk of our wood needs, but as resources are running thin in these regions, tropical forests are quickly being cut to fill the gap.

When considered as wood, or timber, tree species are divided into softwoods and hardwoods. The softwoods are the coniferous, or cone-bearing trees—pine, fir, and spruce. The hardwoods are the broad-leaved flowering trees, like maple oak, ash, hickory, beech, and elm.

A plantation worker in Malaysia collects sap from a rubber tree. The sap will be processed to make rubber for a variety of products.

Softwoods like pine are often used for building materials. Hardwoods tend to be used for making furniture and flooring. Not all softwoods are soft, nor are all hardwoods hard. The wood of the yew, a coniferous softwood tree, is actually harder than most hardwoods. And the wood of poplar and willow trees—both hardwoods—is softer than most softwoods.

Trees and other plants are useful to humans in countless ways. Extremely important but easily taken for granted, trees perform a vital function in filtering rainwater before it reaches reservoirs. Many natural impurities as well as human-made pollutants are naturally converted to harmless substances by soil organisms. Some of the cleanest drinking water comes from lakes or reservoirs surrounded by forest buffers—the larger the buffers, the greater potential for clean water.

Forests of the World

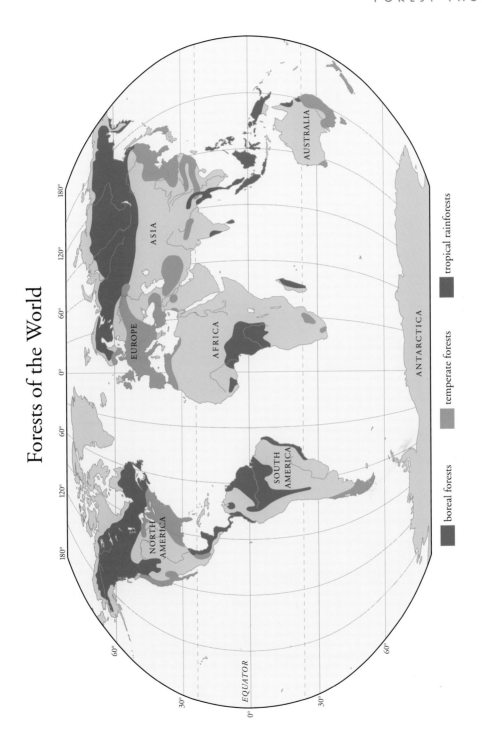

ANTARCTICA

tropical rainforests

temperate forests

boreal forests

Coastal redwoods are among the largest trees in the world. The shady woods they create still provide enough sun for plants like rhododendrons to grow beneath them.

2

WHAT MAKES A FOREST?

Forests are much more than the sum of their parts—trees, shrubs, herbs, ferns, mosses, fungi, soil, insects, herbivores, and carnivores. They are complex, interdependent systems where every life-form fills a role. Plants are the major components of forests, both in number and weight. They can be divided into four broad groups.

The 23,000 species of bryophytes include mosses, hornworts, and liverworts. These small, spreading plants are tolerant of a wide range of conditions, often capable of colonizing rocks, frozen slopes, tree bark, and even bones. One of the best-known members of this group, sphagnum moss, is found in bogs and has amazing water-absorbing capabilities. Like all bryophytes, mosses absorb water directly from their surrounding environment, from rainwater and from the air.

The next two groups, gymnosperms and angiosperms, differ from the bryophytes in that they are vascular plants. This means they have cells that serve as internal conducting vessels for water and other nutrients that they absorb from the soil. They also reproduce using seeds. Many gymnosperms bear their seeds exposed on cones. *Gymnos* is Greek for "naked" and *sperma* means "seed." These types of seeds are considered naked because they are not enclosed in fruits. The coniferous trees like pines, spruces, firs, hemlocks, redwoods, and cedars, as well as cycads and gingkoes, are members of this group, which numbers over 1,000 species.

Angiosperms, or flowering plants, reproduce by making seeds enclosed in ovaries (which develop into fruits) within a flower structure. *Angeion*, the root of *angio-*, is Greek for "vessel," meaning the fruit that carries the seed. The structure of flowers varies widely, as do their sizes. The largest flower in the world is that of *Rafflesia arnoldii*, a tropical parasitic plant whose flower measures more than 3 feet (0.9 meters) across. Some of the smallest flowers are only 0.1 inch (0.25 centimeters) wide and grow in clusters sometimes containing hundreds of individual flowers. Many more species of plants—more than 250,000—are members of the angiosperm group. Broad-leaved deciduous (meaning they drop their leaves seasonally) trees and shrubs, wildflowers, grasses, orchids, palms, cacti, and others are included in this group.

The ferns and fern allies, include some of the world's most primitive plants. While ferns are vascular plants and have leaves similar to those of trees and wildflowers, they reproduce using spores. This group includes ferns, horsetails, and club mosses.

The Rafflesia arnoldii *plant from Sumatra and Borneo lives as a parasite on vines and has no leaves, stems, or roots. It takes twelve months to form and is only open for a few days.*

TREES

As anyone familiar with forests knows, trees are the most obvious and one of the most important parts of the forest. The trees in different biomes all have different characteristics, but they do share a basic common structure. They are tall, usually single-stemmed woody plants with many branches holding a crown of leaves. Like most plants, trees start their lives either from shoots growing directly from roots or a cut stump or as seeds shed from a mature tree.

When the seed sprouts, a shoot grows quickly skyward while roots dig into the earth, anchoring the plant and absorbing water and nutrients. Instead of dying back each year, like herbaceous (non-woody) annual plants, perennial tree stems become hard, and a new layer of growth is added every year just under the surface. The hard outer shell, or bark, keeps the plant from drying out. As the tree grows, the inner layers, or heartwood, die and provide structural support. In temperate biome trees, these layers are visible in cut wood as rings because trees stop growing in the cold season. The first growth layer formed in spring is paler than the layer formed in summer. This clearly shows each year's growth and allows researchers to tell the age of trees and even what the environmental conditions were like each year.

Oak acorns, like most seeds, contain all the nutrients the developing sprout will need to start growing when temperature and moisture conditions are favorable.

17

Plant Reproduction

Not all plants make more plants in the same way. Many plants in the boreal and temperate forest biomes, as well as upper canopy trees in the tropical forest, are wind-pollinated, meaning that wind carries the pollen from plant to plant. This may seem a haphazard way to reproduce, but plants increase their chances by creating billions of pollen grains each season. When the pollen from the male flower contacts the female flower, fertilization occurs and a seed begins to form.

Other plants get help from animals. Many creatures, mostly insects, feed on the nectar produced in flowers. This substance is created by trees and other plants specifically for the nourishment of these creatures. In turn, these pollinators help the immobile plants reproduce. As a bee, for example, lands on a flower to extract its nectar, tiny pollen grains are caught in the small hairs on the bee's head, body, and legs. As the bee moves from male flower to female flower, the pollen is transferred, effectively making it possible for the plants to mate and reproduce. This is a much more efficient system than wind pollination, and plants that rely on animal pollination don't have to produce nearly as much pollen. Other animals that pollinate flowers include flies, moths, hummingbirds, and bats.

When the weather, damage to the plant, or other environmental conditions prevent pollination or flower formation, some plants add to the pollen and seed strategy by reproducing by vegetative means. Plants such as aspen trees, many vines, and some grasses can sprout new shoots from their roots. These new plants are clones of the original—their genetic material is exactly the same as the original plant—so most species that reproduce this way can't rely entirely on this method.

If they did, they might eventually die out due to a lack of genetic diversity. Mating with other individuals of the same species is the only way to ensure that their genetic makeup remains diverse and healthy.

Pine trees are wind-pollinated. The male flowers produce pollen, which is picked up and carried by the wind and hopefully makes contact with nearby female flowers.

The strong, hard wood of trees is what makes them able to grow so tall. Height is a great advantage, allowing trees to gather more sunlight for photosynthesis. This improves their growth, helps them disperse their seeds more widely, and makes their flowers available to a wider variety of pollinators. Among the tallest trees in the world, the coastal redwoods of California can reach heights close to 400 feet (122 m). The great size of trees also means that there is more surface area to lose oxygen and water to the air. As a result, trees are constantly working to replace these essential resources.

Trees can be very long-lived organisms. On one side of the age scale are the birches, which usually live about 60 to 90 years. In contrast, one individual tree of the bristlecone pine species was aged at about 4,900 years.

Trees also provide shelter and shade for all the creatures and plants that live beneath them. The environment they create limits the amount of wind, water, snow, sunlight, and cold beneath the canopy—the upper layer of tree crowns—and on the ground. This keeps many of the organisms living there protected from drying, freezing, or being flooded out.

CYCLES AND INTERACTIONS

But forests are not simply a collection of trees and other plants. Forests are places where recycling occurs continuously and is absolutely necessary to the survival of the whole ecosystem. So the story of forests can't be told without describing their complex interactions with the surrounding environment.

Some scientists consider all ecosystems, biomes, or even the whole biosphere as systems, where each part—trees, fungi, herbivores, carnivores—plays a specific function. There are inputs and outputs to these systems as well, in the form of nutrients, water, dead and decaying parts, and new growth.

Forests are very complex ecological systems that regulate Earth's air supply. In the process called photosynthesis, trees and other plants absorb and convert sunlight, water, and carbon in the form of carbon dioxide (CO_2)—a gas that all animals, including humans, exhale—into carbohydrates (sugars) needed for plant growth. Fortunately for us, when plants recycle CO_2 during photosynthesis, another byproduct is oxygen (O_2). Oxygen is used constantly by plants and animals as they respire, or breathe. Without the careful balance of all these gases in the air, life on Earth would still be primitive and humans may never have evolved.

The essential element carbon is added to the system when plants and animals die. Their decaying bodies return carbon to the soil, which becomes enriched by this input and benefits further plant growth. Some of the carbon is also turned into coal or gas and becomes part of Earth's crust and atmosphere.

Plants also help cycle water through the environment. As rain, water is absorbed into the soil and taken up by plants for nourishment and to fuel the photosynthetic process. Excess water that runs off the land flows into streams and rivers, which then flow into lakes or oceans. Some of this water evaporates into the air and later falls again as rain.

Nitrates, another important nutrient for trees, are used to make proteins for cell growth. Nitrates can't be absorbed and converted by trees directly from the nitrogen in the atmosphere, but microorganisms like bacteria and fungi in the soil can do the work for them. In return, the leaf, branch, and bark litter that drop from trees to the ground are food for soil organisms including fungi, bacteria, worms, snails, and protozoa. These creatures create the rich soil layer that billions of different organisms utilize.

Plants are also important for herbivores, or animals that eat plants exclusively. Many members of the animal kingdom, from mice, rabbits, and birds to deer, buffalo, and even elephants, rely on plant leaves, stems, roots, and seeds for their survival. However, these creatures don't

A jaguar stalks its prey in the Costa Rican rainforest.

simply take from their environment. They are part of a cycle as well. Herbivores may be killed and eaten by carnivores like wolves and lions. The droppings of all these animals gradually decompose—again through the action of bacteria, fungi, and insects—with the remnants becoming part of the soil layer. When herbivores and other animals die, their bodies are transformed by the same processes of decomposition into minerals and nutrients that enrich the soil.

FUNGI

There are approximately 100,000 known species of fungi in the world, and scientists estimate that there may be as many as 200,000 more yet undiscovered. Many of them are associated with forested environments. Some books lump these organisms in with plants, but recent DNA studies show that fungi are no more similar to plants than they are to animals.

Fungi are one of the five main kingdoms of life on Earth. They don't depend on photosynthesis, like plants, but take their nutrients directly from plants and other organisms. They range in size from microscopic to many feet across. There are many arguments in the scientific community about what constitutes the size of an individual fungus.

Most people think that the mushroom is the main part of a fungus. But it is in fact just the fruiting body, or reproductive organ, of the whole organism. Below ground or inside a rotting log is the root system, more properly known as the mycelium. The many segments of the mycelium, called hyphae, are branches that spread through the ground, pulling in moisture and nutrients and doing the actual work of decomposition. These netlike growths can extend over a vast area.

One fungus found below ground in and around the Blue Mountains of eastern Oregon covers 2,200 acres (890 ha) of land. That's roughly equal to 1,665 U. S. football fields. Estimated to be about 2,400 years old, this fungus is harmful to trees, attacking their roots. But this is just another process of regeneration in the forest. New trees and other plants will crop up in place of the dead trees. And the lifeless snags, or dead trees, provide perches for birds and food for insects. Clusters of golden mushrooms appear from this fungus in the fall.

In most cases, the above-ground mushrooms only appear for a few days of the year. When moisture conditions are favorable, they quickly

A fungus spreads across a rotting log, forming a netlike pattern.

appear, swell to their full size, and release their spores—their mode of reproduction—into the wind to be carried to a suitable site for a new fungus to grow.

Kinds of Fungi

There are three main groups of fungi. Decomposers are those that process the huge quantities of plant debris and animal waste that collect in the forest. Without mushrooms, molds, rusts, and other fungi to continuously process the litter from forests, most plants would be smothered by the accumulated debris. Plants also benefit from the rich soil that decomposition produces, continuing the cycle of growth. Some insects even farm fungus, providing their waste for the fungi's growth and harvesting the fruiting bodies for food.

Mycorrhizae are fungi that take their relationship with plants one step further. Their mycelia actually surround tree rootlets, directly transferring much-needed nutrients to the tree while the tree provides waste products for the fungi. This mutually beneficial relationship, known as mutualism, occurs with a large number of tree species, especially in environments where trees have a difficult time getting the nutrients they need.

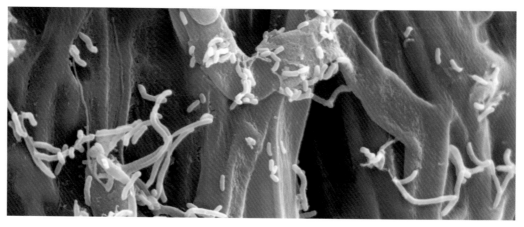

Mycorrhizae (fungi) form around the roots of their hosts, providing the plant with nutrients, while absorbing moisture and waste from the host.

A killer fungus grows on a weevil in a Costa Rican forest. The fungus will eventually take over the insect's body and kill it.

Scientists have found that some tree species will not grow well in a new environment—for example, in a tree plantation—unless the mycorrhizae that the tree is normally associated with is put into the soil to form that special relationship.

Howecer not all relationships with fungi are beneficial to the host plant or animal. Parasitic fungi can actually kill, taking what they need and depleting the host so much that it dies. Some insects eat spores, which then grow inside the insect's body, killing it and eventually developing into a fruiting body, or mushroom. Other species attach themselves to living trees, slowly breaking down the woody cells, and interrupting the flow of nutrients through the tree. This eventually results in the death of the tree.

A few species of fungi even glow in the dark. One species in particular is grown and maintained by astronauts on NASA space missions because of its sensitivity to toxins in the air. If the air is toxic, the fungus will cease to luminesce, or glow. If, during a routine check, the lights are turned off and the fungi are no longer glowing, the astronauts will know to look for the source of the toxin.

Cooksonia pertoni is one of the world's oldest vascular platns. This fossil is more than 400 million years old.

3

EVOLUTION OF FORESTS

When plants first appeared on Earth, they looked nothing like the plants familiar to most people today. They actually evolved in the sea as single-celled, algae-like organisms. Over time, they became more complex, evolving into multi-celled organisms and then into seaweeds. Plants obviously cover Earth today, but a billion years ago there was no oxygen in the air, no ozone layer to protect them from ultraviolet rays, and no organic material in the soil to support them. Slowly, as the first primitive plants began to colonize land, they began to add oxygen and ozone to the atmosphere. This protective layer around the planet enabled other life-forms to take hold on land. By 500 million years ago, a diversity of primitive life abounded.

The first vascular plants evolved about 440 million years ago in the Silurian period. By the Carboniferous period, about 345 million years ago, there were forests of 100-foot-tall (30-meter-tall), treelike club mosses and ferns. Gradually, drier and warmer conditions of the Permian period favored other plant life and caused these trees to begin to evolve into their relatively tiny descendants that we know from today's forests.

The first seed plants appeared around this same time, and the first trees—the gymnosperms—evolved about 280 million years ago, in the late Paleozoic period. These early trees had few edible parts, so there was little animal life in these forests.

Angiosperms, or flowering plants, evolved around 125 million years ago, in the Cretaceous period. They adapted easily to changing climates and spread throughout the world, pushing the gymnosperms to colder and drier environments. Temperate and tropical forests became widespread by about 65 million years ago, during the Tertiary period.

The arrival and evolution of flowering plants prompted a profusion of new animal life-forms that evolved to take advantage of the new nutrient-rich food source—the seeds, fruits, and nectar. Many of these creatures were arboreal, living in the trees. Over millions of years, many animals have become closely associated with particular types of plants. In some cases, certain moths, bees, bats, and other creatures have become the only pollinators of certain plant species.

GLACIAL TIMES

While many of the trees in the forest biome that we know today had evolved by the beginning of the Pleistocene epoch, about 2 million years ago, changes taking place due to a warming and cooling climate shifted things around a bit. Beginning about 1.6 million years ago, Earth was subject to about sixteen to twenty cooling and warming trends that caused glacial ice from the poles to advance (grow) southward and retreat (shrink) northward. Populations of both plants and animals began to migrate and change in response. Closer to the edge of the glacial ice, conifers like spruce and fir were able to expand their range in cold times, pushing warm-loving plants, like many deciduous trees, southward. During the warmer interglacial periods, as the glacial edge retreated northward, these southern species also followed.

The last cool period reached its maximum about 16,500 years ago in North America. As the conifers retreated northward for the last time, they left behind remnants of their populations on isolated peaks in places like the Appalachian Mountains. Conditions at these high elevations were still favorable for conifer growth, even though these trees were south of their main populations. Also left behind were animal species that lived in these environments, like the black-capped chickadee and the northern flying squirrel.

The deciduous trees that now occupy the temperate forest biome began moving into their current territory about 12,500 years ago. While many tree species survived these climate changes, others didn't do as well. The hickories, for example, familiar and important forest trees in eastern North America, became extinct in Europe and Asia due to the many changes in climate.

And some species of animals couldn't survive the change to a warm climate cycle. Mastodons, mammoths, saber-toothed cats, and dire wolves became extinct during the transition from the Pleistocene period to the Holocene, our current period of time.

RECENT FOREST HISTORY

Many changes brought on by humans occurred more recently in geologic time, and this is also part of the history of forests. Even the earliest humans influenced forests through their resource needs. Native Americans cleared land in the temperate forest for farms, usually by burning the forest. They used fire to create better hunting grounds for deer, turkey, and other forest-edge-loving species. As human populations grew, the demand for wood and productive agricultural lands prompted much more intensive cutting.

Forest Histories

Scientists use many techniques to learn about the history of the world's forests. Learning about the oldest forests may be the hardest task. But luckily, many clues are left behind.

When trees fall into bogs or swamps, the anaerobic (oxygen-poor) environments don't allow them to decay. In some cases, the wood is slowly replaced by minerals, forming exact replicas of the trees, inside and out, called fossils. Or the trees may form an impression in the surrounding sediment, which later turns to rock, creating a lasting mold.

There have been many fluctuations in tree species populations during the Holocene period (from two million years ago to the present). One technique that scientists use to reveal these changes is called pollen analysis. This helps them to figure out which plant species lived at certain times in history. In bogs and ponds, soil, leaves, and pollen grains accumulate over thousands of years, forming a new layer every year. Scientists drive long, hollow, metal tubes deep into the sediment below the water's surface. Then they pull out the tubes and remove the sediment core. Scientists can count back from the top of the core, which represents our present time, and match different layers to different years, counting pollen grains along the way. This gives them a sense of what the forests looked like. If there was more pine pollen than hardwood pollen in a given period, then it is possible that pines were the dominant tree species during that time.

Ages of specific trees—and consequently of whole forests—can be determined by a technique known as tree ring analysis. The age of a temperate forest tree can be determined by simply counting the seasonal growth rings along a cross-section near the tree's base. They are visible as light and dark stripes only when the tree is cut down and you can read the rings across the stump or when a tree core is taken from a living tree. This involves screwing a slender hollow tube through the bark and into the tree's center. After unscrewing the tube and then removing the core, the rings can be counted.

The outer rings are the newest growth, while the inner rings are the oldest. Not only can scientists tell the age of a tree this way, they can also estimate what the climate was like in a particular year or whether the tree experienced some kind of stress. If the rings are wide in a given year, it means there was a lot of rain then, prompting more growth. If the ring is unusually narrow, that means the year was dry, restricting the tree's growth. If there is a hollow spot or charcoal within the rings, this indicates that a fire scarred the tree some time in its past.

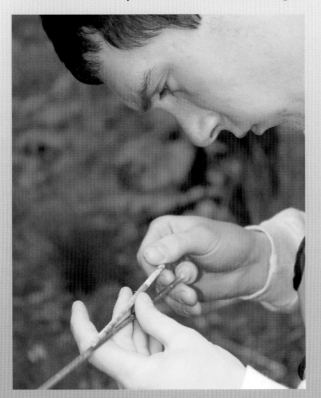

A core sample is taken to determine a tree's age.

The practice of clear-cutting, where all trees in a stand are cut, is a controversial logging method. Many in the logging industry see it as an efficient, low-cost method, while many environmentalists cite the loss of soil and damage to waterways when trees are abruptly removed, as well as the drastic change in wildlife habitat.

From 80 to 90 percent of the original forests in the northeastern United States were cut between the seventeenth and nineteenth centuries. Where the forest did grow back, the collection of trees and animals was not quite the same.

While most tropical forests were not subject to the settlement pressures and deforestation that the temperate forests have undergone in previous centuries, they are experiencing it now at a much more accelerated pace. The United Nations' 2000 Global Forest Resource Assessment calculated that 1 percent, or 35.1 million acres (14.2 million ha), of tropical rainforests were lost worldwide each year between 1990 and 2000.

Other forest types have experienced intensive resource extraction. The boreal forest, with its vast areas of quality softwood timber, has undergone extensive logging over the years. This area has also been exploited for its rich oil and gas deposits as well as its water resources.

All these recent changes to forest biomes came about primarily because people found forests to be very rich places to live, full of good soils, plentiful food, tall trees, and many other valuable resources. In a very short time—geologically speaking—humans have dramatically changed Earth's forests.

A grizzly uses a spruce tree to scratch an itch.

4

BOREAL FORESTS

If we start in the North, the first forested biome we encounter is the boreal forest. It stretches around the globe in a belt across North America and Eurasia, overlying areas that were once covered by glaciers. A vast area of mostly coniferous trees, the boreal forest, provides an incalculable service to the biosphere by processing huge amounts of CO_2, helping to keep the atmosphere in balance. The North American expression includes parts of Alaska and most of northern Canada, while the Eurasian expression includes Scandinavia (Norway, Sweden, and Finland), and most of Siberia in Russia, where the boreal forest is known by its Russian name, taiga. The Siberian taiga is the largest forest in the world, larger than the entire area of the United States.

Bitterly cold winters and cool summers in the boreal forest make for a very short growing season: there are only 60 to 150 frost-free days annually in this biome. Snow covers the frozen ground most of the winter. The summer is a very wet time that fosters a lot of growth, especially in the insect world. Mosquitoes and black flies hatch out in great numbers.

Low year-round temperatures limit the amount of bacterial activity in the soil. Thus there is not much decomposition and a relatively deep layer of tree litter on the ground. When the tough, waxy conifer needles do break down, they mostly add organic acids to the soil. This leaches the iron and other minerals away from the soil layer, leaving a bleached, grayish upper soil layer. Despite the relatively low level of biodiversity compared to other biomes, the Canadian boreal forest is home to the largest (wood bison) and the smallest (pygmy shrew) mammals in North America.

BOREAL FOREST PLANTS

The cold temperatures and acidic soils make for a relatively low level of diversity in the boreal forest biome. The two major expressions, the North American and the Eurasian, have similar tree types, but the species are different. Conifers predominate, and there is a wide diversity of these, including various species of spruce, fir, pine, and larch. Pines are found on the drier, sandier soils while the spruces grow on the denser,

Conifers, trees that do not lose their leaves, thrive on the lower slopes of this mountain range in Alaska. Their slender, conical shape allows them to shed snow easily.

The floor of a boreal forest may include bearberry, bluberry, or crowberry bushes.

heavier soils. Plants and animals that live in such a harsh environment have evolved special ways to deal with the cold temperatures and heavy snows. The shape of most boreal forest coniferous trees is itself a special adaptation to snow. Firs have the ultimate design. Their conical shape, with branches hanging down toward the ground, allows easy shedding of heavy snow, which prevents branches from snapping off.

Conifer trees' stiff, waxy needles hold water better than wide, deciduous leaves. This is especially important when the ground is frozen most of the year, preventing trees from taking up water. The dark color of the needles helps absorb heat well, and since conifers don't have to put new leaves on every spring, they can get started photosynthesizing as soon as temperatures are warm enough.

Along the northern edge of the biome, the trees tend to be stunted by the increasingly colder, drier, and more windswept conditions. Where there has been disturbance to plant cover and soil—by flooding, wind, or fire, for example—hardwoods like willow, birch, alder, and aspen can more quickly colonize the area than conifers can. Once these deciduous trees become larger and shade the ground, the conifer seedlings can then take hold. They continue to grow slowly, staying small, until the short-lived hardwoods die, opening up a gap in the canopy. This provides space and light for the conifers to grow, quickly filling in the canopy gap.

Only a few acid-loving, low, trailing shrub species like bearberry, crowberry, and bilberry are able to grow in the shady, acidic understory (the lower level of a forest) below the mature conifers. But mosses and lichens are common here because they have adapted to the low-light, low-nutrient conditions there.

BOREAL FOREST ANIMALS

Many animals of this biome are heavily furred, like the lynx and its main prey, the snowshoe hare. The arctic fox, whose fur changes from reddish in the summer to pure white in the winter, also feeds on the hares. There are many weasels, including mink, ermine, pine marten, sable, fisher,

A mink hunts for food along the forest floor.

Because of their large size, Eurasian eagle-owls can hunt a variety of prey, from insects to small deer.

and wolverine. These predators survive on the large and irruptive populations (meaning they rise and fall steeply at regular intervals) of lemmings, voles, red squirrels, and other herbivorous rodents.

Snowshoe hare populations explode and crash on a ten-year cycle. Scientists believe that this dynamic helps stabilize the populations of predator and prey. If the numbers of snowshoe hares were stable all the time, the numbers of lynx would be stable and might increase until they hunted all the hares to extinction. In their ten-year-cycle when hares' numbers drop, it causes a drop in the lynx population, but on a delayed cycle. The numbers of lynx are lower in the next year when the hare population explodes. This ensures that the low numbers of lynx will be unable to catch all the new hares.

Hawks are one of the major diurnal (daytime-hunting) predators in this biome. The northern goshawk breeds here, raising its young on the summer profusion of small mammal and bird life. Nocturnal (nighttime) hunters like the northern hawk-owl and the Eurasian eagle

A bull moose forages in a boreal forest in Alaska.

owl take the place of the hawks at night, feeding on the same prey. In addition to the supply of small rodents, these birds will also kill young deer and foxes.

Frequenting the many streams, rivers, and lakes in this biome are beavers, mink, otters, and muskrats. The beaver effects the ecology of the forests near waterways by building dams and flooding these areas, killing trees and thereby promoting different types of plant growth, like hardwood trees, grasses, and shrubs.

Along the northern limits of the boreal forest biome in North America, muskoxen and caribou range in herds, feeding on mosses and lichens, as do reindeer, their counterparts in Eurasia. Other large herbivores, such as moose and elk, frequent the swampy areas farther south. Wolves and bears are the top predators. Wolves are true carnivores; bears will eat a variety of foods.

Coping with the Cold

Some mammal species and most insects cannot survive the severe cold and deep snow of the boreal forest winter. Most creatures employ one of three strategies for coping with these conditions: migration, hibernation, or resistance.

Birds are the main group of migrating animals. Many species, like the warblers, breed in the north, taking advantage of the abundance of food and nest sites available in the summer months. Songbirds catch great numbers of insects that hatch at the onset of spring, and they gather abundant seeds from various species of conifer to feed their developing chicks.

After the breeding season, when young birds have left the nest to fend for themselves, many species travel south to tropical forests, where food is plentiful. When the temperatures drop and the snow falls in the boreal forest, there is precious little food available; the insects have either died out or become dormant for the winter, and the conifers have dropped their seeds. Just a small number of bird species can endure the winter here.

Only a few mammals actually hibernate, or go dormant for the winter, in order to wait out the cold temperatures and lack of food. Bears, for example, spend most of the winter months in their dens, either small caves or large hollow trees. By slowing their metabolism to the point where they are not using much energy, they are able to go for months without eating, urinating, or defecating. They prepare for this period of inactivity by fattening up in the weeks before the cold weather. Female bears do, however, give birth during this dormant period. The cubs will stay in the den with their mother, suckling and being largely inactive as well.

Most reptiles and amphibians have no choice but to hibernate, since they are cold-blooded creatures, unable to regulate their own body temperature. Many snakes, salamanders, and frogs find a safe, dark place to spend the winter. Groups of mixed species of snakes will gather in rock dens. Toads will burrow into the soft earth to protect themselves from the freezing temperatures. Frogs usually burrow into the mud of stream beds, as do salamanders and turtles.

But many organisms must stay and endure the harsh conditions of winter in the frozen north. The larval and pupal stages of some insects

The pine grosbeak—a true boreal species of finch—prefers coniferous forests and the seeds and fruits from spruce, pine, and juniper, as well as deciduous species.

produce a sort of antifreeze that prevents them from being injured or killed by freezing liquids in their bodies.

Many seed-eating birds like nutcrackers, crossbills, grosbeaks, pine siskins, and redpolls stick around for the winter. But even these birds are forced to head south in years when the trees don't produce much seed.

The mammals that stay active in winter have adapted ways of dealing with cold and snow. Lynx, and snowshoe hare have developed larger feet to enable them to walk on top of the snow. Moose can lift their long legs shoulder high, stepping easily through even deep snow.

PEOPLE OF BOREAL FORESTS

Because of the bitterly cold winters, fewer humans live in this biome than in other forested biomes. Most of the larger cities of Canada are south of the boreal forest, so the forest itself has not seen much major settlement. There are smaller towns, villages, and even trading posts to handle the trade in pelts from the many furred mammals.

But these Canadian forests are home to nearly one million indigenous, or native, people—about 80 percent of Canada's indigenous population. Some of these communities are directly dependent on the forest for their basic needs and livelihood and most have a strong cultural connection to the land.

The boreal forest and the taiga also contain some of the most valuable timber in the world, providing Canada and Russia with a steady supply of trees for their pulp wood and paper industries. Canada is also the world's largest exporter of wood products; their economy is heavily dependent on the timber resources. Seventy percent of wood exports are sold to the United States. Many of the logging practices in this region and the Eurasian taiga are intensive and unsustainable; they include clear-cutting, heavy pesticide use, and conversion of natural forests to plantations. Oil and gas exploration, as well as more than 300 hydroelectric dams in the region, have also harmed the forests and fragmented wildlife habitat.

But the native communities allied with environmental groups are working to protect the forests of this region through public education and working with organizations to promote change in the logging industry. Unfortunately, because of the Canadian government's economic dependence on these various resources, there has been a lot of resistance to the strict conservation measures intended to protect the forests.

The Trans-Siberia Railway, which travels from Moscow in far western Russia to Vladivostok on the Sea of Japan, has helped to open this vast area of the Eurasian taiga to tourism and trade. Irkutsk is the major city in the region. It originally served as a trading stop on the Angara River between China and eastern Russia. More recently, its proximity to Lake Baikal, the largest lake in Eurasia and the deepest lake in the world, makes it a popular tourist destination.

Temperate forests, especially the eastern deciduous forest of the United States, display vivid autumn colors as the trees slow photosynthesis and withdraw water and nutrients from their leaves in preparation for winter.

5

TEMPERATE FORESTS

Temperate forests cover only 6 percent of Earth's surface, but some of the most populated and well-developed areas occur in and around them, on large continental land masses in the Northern Hemisphere.

Temperate forests are found where the growing season, or the period of time that a plant can grow in a particular region, is long (approximately six months), warm, and humid. The temperate climate causes wide fluctuations in temperature, from -22 degrees Fahrenheit (-30 ° Celsius) in midwinter to 86 °F (30 °C) in summer. Precipitation occurs throughout the year and can total from 20 to 65 inches (50 to 165 cm), depending upon local conditions. As in the boreal forest biome, the cold temperatures create a type of drought, causing plants to become inactive. But the snow cover helps to insulate tree roots from the freezing and potentially fatal winter temperatures.

The major expressions of this biome occur in North America, Europe, and Asia. In eastern North America, the forest extends as far northward as southern Canada and the Great Lakes, eastward to the Atlantic Coast, south to southern Florida and the Gulf Coast, and west to the Mississippi River. This is the most intact example of this type of

A hidden waterfall breaks up a forest in North Carolina's Great Smokey Mountains.

forest in the world, even though most of the trees have been cut at least once, and it contains the greatest diversity of all temperate broadleaf forests. (This name refers to the relatively wide, flat leaves that most trees in this biome have, which are ideal for collecting the maximum amount of sunlight in the few months they are on the trees.) The biodiversity of the Great Smokey Mountains in Tennessee and North Carolina is so great, for example, that this region was designated a World Biosphere Reserve in 1976 and a World Heritage Site in 1983.

Where the temperate forest exists in western and northern Europe, the species composition is less diverse. While the types of trees are similar to those in North America, many species became extinct during the Ice Ages, leaving only a few representatives of each type. Within recent human history, many European forests have been converted to forest plantations or cleared for agriculture, as in China and Japan.

China has been settled for so long that farms have covered the countryside for the last 4,000 years. The kinds of trees and other plants that the farms replaced are known only from the fossil record. But the mountains of Korea still harbor some natural forest. The composition is similar to that of the temperate broadleaf forests of North America.

TEMPERATE FOREST PLANTS

The temperate forest biome fosters a broad diversity of trees, including various species of oak, maple, beech, birch, ash, hickory, basswood, elm, willow, holly, and magnolia. Perhaps the most recognizable tree is the sugar maple because of its blazing red, orange, and yellow autumn colors.

This color change signals the end of the growing season in temperate forests. Many of the trees here are deciduous, meaning they drop their leaves every fall. This is a mechanism trees use to conserve energy and reduce damage to their branches over the sometimes long winters. While deciduous trees do not actually become dormant during this period, they do slow their growth functions and do not photosynthesize.

This image shows three species of birch tree from the temperate forest: paper or white birch has peeling white bark; gray birch has a light silvery bark; black or sweet birch has dark, shiny bark, and its sap has been used to make drinks.

Springtime in the temperate forest brings out leaves and flowers of trees, like this bitternut hickory with it's heavy load of catkins, or male reproductive parts, from which pollen will emerge.

In the spring, when temperatures become just warm enough, the flower and leaf buds that were formed the previous summer will swell and open. Flowers and leaves grow quickly to begin the reproductive and photosynthetic processes. In the fall, many tree species drop their seeds or let the wind carry them to ground favorable for germination. The heavier seeds, like oak acorns, provide food (also known as mast) for many woodland creatures, such as deer and squirrels.

There are many layers in temperate forests. In addition to the canopy trees (up to 100 feet, or 30 m, tall), there is usually a layer of "suppressed" trees below the tall ones. (These can be the same species as above or different species that are shade-tolerant, or better able to compete under the low-light conditions.) While they have the ability to achieve the same heights as the dominant canopy trees, suppressed trees are limited in their growth because the canopy trees are using up the light, space, and nutrients they need. When canopy trees die, the suppressed trees can grow into the canopy.

Below the suppressed tree layer is the small tree layer, which consists of young canopy species as well as species that never attain great height but can grow to 30 to 40 feet (10 to 13 m) tall. These small trees include dogwoods, redbud, serviceberry, hornbeams, and hop-hornbeams.

Beneath the small trees is the shrub layer which is equally diverse and, depending upon the habitat, may include members of the heath family, such as rhododendron, azalea, mountain laurel, blueberry, and huckleberry.

In the early spring the lack of leaf cover benefits the many beautiful woodland wildflowers—such as bloodroot, trillium, wild ginger, Dutchman's breeches, violets, and hepatica—that grow along the ground. These non-woody plants complete most of their yearly life cycle in those few short weeks before the trees once again put their roof of leaves over the forest for the summer. This spring flush of flowers is an important food source for the many insects, bats, and birds that help to pollinate and thus spread these species across the landscape.

The ground layer in this biome is similar to the boreal forests, with various species of mosses, lichens, and club mosses covering rocks and

the shaded open ground. The dropped leaves, bark, fruit, and flowers of the many different plants are what create the rich soils in this biome. The greatest plant diversity occurs on the richest soils, which hold moisture well but are not too wet. Drier, sandier soils may promote a less diverse but distinctive community of pine trees, scrub oak, and other drought-tolerant vegetation.

Dutchman's breeches—the flowers shown here—grow on rocky, forested slopes with rich, moist, undisturbed soils in eastern North America. Many think that the flowers resemble white pants.

Phenology

For almost as long as humans have been around, they have been fascinated by the growth of plants. In particular, the yearly renewal of life in the temperate forests, where the showy spring floral display occurs in a relatively short period of time, has been the object of much scientific study.

Scientific research into phenology—the study of periodic natural events, including animal migration and breeding cycles, as well as plant growth—in the last couple hundred years has focused on lilac bushes as well as many other native species. Some of these records cover decades and in a few cases, centuries of plant growth. This information can tell us about the biology of different species and how they react to specific environmental conditions, including climate, soil type, moisture levels, and even pollution. Research suggests that the trigger for flowering and leafing of temperate plants is related to the accumulation of warmth, known as heat sums, in the spring. Each species and possibly even each individual plant has its own heat-sum level that it reacts to for each process.

One study of native woodland plants in a central Massachusetts forest has recorded twenty-five years of spring plant growth, including leafing and flowering, of shrubs and trees. This information has helped researchers paint a picture of the variations in the growth of these species, both from year to year and from location to location within the study site. This information is also helpful in comparing growth rates to other locations around the world. Long-term records of plant growth together with temperature and other climate data give scientists a baseline. They use this baseline to measure many things, including the effects of the changing global climate on local plant life.

This type of study has shown that certain temperate trees, like beech for example, actually evolved in a more tropical climate but migrated north as the glaciers retreated, staking their claim among today's temperate forest trees. Beech trees are more like tropical trees in their spring leafing: They react to length of daylight, not accumulated warmth. Researchers have even seen, within the last century, a movement of plant populations farther north as global temperatures appear to climb due to fossil fuel pollution.

The timing of these events can be connected to other events in the natural world as well. Many woodland herbivores and insects time their reproduction, foraging, and hibernation to coincide with the availability of their preferred food source, such as acorns. As a matter of fact, these events are often influenced by and even dependent on each other. In lean mast years, squirrels may not do well, and many may die, while in a good mast year, squirrel populations may increase to take advantage of the food source.

T E M P E R A T E   F O R E S T   A N I M A L S

The wide diversity of tree species in the temperate forest biome provides abundant food and cover for a varied array of wildlife. Herbivores include white-tailed deer, flying squirrels, chipmunks, and woodland mice. These creatures are dependent on the summer plant growth; they feed on leaves, fruits, and nuts.

While the winters in this biome are not as severe as those of the boreal forest, the cold temperatures and snow are enough to cause some creatures to migrate or hibernate for the season. Squirrels, chipmunks, and other rodents deal with the scarcity of food in the winter by caching their food in burrows (chipmunks) or in holes they dig in the ground and in hollows in trees (squirrels). Woodland mice that learn to spend the winter in people's houses often store nuts and seeds in shoes. Deer don't have this option—they have to survive the winter by eating the twigs and bark of trees or any leftover vegetation they can dig up from beneath the snow.

Flying squirrels are one of the more unusual and also rarely seen creatures of the North American temperate forest. They leap and glide from tree to tree at night using the skin flaps on the sides of their bodies as "wings."

These young red foxes, a common animal of the temperate and boreal forests, are sticking close to their burrow, waiting for their mother to bring them the morning meal.

Omnivores include foxes, raccoons, opossums, skunks, and black bears. These creatures are less likely to be hurt by poor mast years, lack of fruit, or low fish or rodent numbers because they can easily switch to an alternate food source. As a result these are some of the most successful mammals in the temperate forest.

Many of the carnivores that have historically inhabited this biome were killed or driven out of the western region, but they have included timber wolves, mountain lions, and bobcats. With the removal of these meat-eaters, the opportunistic coyote, a native of the western grasslands and deserts, has moved into the area and become very successful. Wintertime is lean for carnivores, too. They wait until warm, sunny days awaken the rodents hibernating deep in the snow pack. Rodents emerge slow and groggy—easy pickings for hungry predators.

Hawks, eagles, and owls are common predators in this biome, profiting from the wide diversity of rodent and small mammal life. Red-tailed hawks, one of the more successful diurnal raptors in North America, can adapt to many different environments, moving between woodland edges and grasslands. They soar above these areas, watching for any movement. After spotting a rabbit or some other small mammal, they dive down quickly, snapping their prey's neck or piercing their vital organs with razor-sharp talons. Other raptors in this biome include the Cooper's hawk, American kestrel, Eurasian kestrel, bald eagle, and golden eagle.

After dusk, owls hunt many of the same rodent species that hawks hunt during the day. They sit silently in trees, relying on their especially sharp hearing to find prey. Once they locate it, the owl's eyes—especially adapted to low-light conditions—take over. They stay focused on the prey as the owl's silent wings carry the raptor swiftly down before seizing the unsuspecting rodent in its strong, sharp talons.

The songbird species that spend the whole year in the temperate forests are mostly seed eaters and omnivores. North American species include the ground-nesting wild turkey; the hairy woodpecker; the treetop-dwelling red-eyed vireo; the hermit thrush; the brightly colored purple finch; and the red-breasted nuthatch, which creeps up and down trees, picking out insects and seeds from tree bark.

In the winter, these resident species either cache their food like squirrels do or subsist on the high-protein leaf and flower buds of trees and shrubs. In North America, blue jays help grow new oak trees by caching acorns in the ground or in old stumps. They often store more acorns than they can eat or find again, so some of these—given the right soil and moisture conditions—will sprout and grow, often far from the parent tree. This is ideal for the oaks, whose heavy seeds cannot travel far without help. And the blue jays have a nutritious diet for the winter.

Woodpeckers are common bird species of forested environments, with 214 species worldwide. This hairy woodpecker is feeding its young in their nest.

Some temperate forest birds are cavity-nesters, meaning they make their nests in holes that they either find in trees or make the holes themselves. Woodpeckers do this by rapidly hammering their large, strong beaks into tree trunks. They have developed special muscles and a dense skull to enable them to withstand the repeated vibrations. These adaptations come in handy when feeding as well, since woodpeckers eat insects that feed upon and nest in trees. Cavity-nesters unable to make their own holes use old, unoccupied woodpecker nests or natural tree cavities.

Migratory temperate forest bird species—warblers, wrens, thrushes, tanagers, and hummingbirds, for example—are only in this biome for the summer breeding season. They make the long journey from tropical areas to take advantage of the abundant food and nesting territories of the temperate forests in summertime. Most of these species are insectivores, eating billions of insects.

Warblers are one of the more numerous bird groups, with 116 species worldwide. They are a particular challenge for birdwatchers to identify because many species have similar plumage. And since they often spend their time in treetops, feeding on the many arboreal insects they are difficult to spot among the leaves.

Most of the amazing variety of insects in temperate forests enter a state of suspended development known as diapause for the winter months. Worms and millipedes react to the cold season by burrowing into the ground. The rich soils, wetlands, and food sources—in the form of insects and small mammals—also support many species of snakes, salamanders, turtles, and frogs.

Salamanders are a very important animal of temperate forests. They are an important link in the food chain, feeding on insects and larvae while in turn being fed upon by mammals and birds.

PEOPLE OF TEMPERATE FORESTS

The favorable climate and rich resources of the temperate forests also support a large population of humans. The great variety of trees, productive soils, streams and rivers and wetlands have provided essential resources for many of the world's most populous and prosperous towns and cities.

Trappers and hunters rely on forest wildlife for food, clothing, sport, and income sources. The wood from the great diversity of tree species is used for all sorts of structures, from large public buildings to chicken coops, as well as furniture, tools, and baseball bats.

People have cleared most of the forests in this biome of trees at least once in their history. In many cases, the land has been converted to farms and forest plantations. Some of the native forests have been allowed to grow back, such as those in many areas of northeastern North America, as farming has shifted to other regions. Some former forestland, such as in China have been so intensely farmed for so long, that they are now useless for growing food crops or trees. It may be a long time, even hundreds of years, before they can support healthy forests again.

Forestry, the science and practice of tree harvesting, is a way of life for people in many regions—the northeastern and the southeastern United States, for example. These areas are working hard to balance the huge demand for wood products with the public's desire for natural area protection, or conservation. Sustainable forestry methods are being explored and employed in these areas. Sustainable practices minimize the impact of tree harvesting on the natural forest communities and help to ensure future supplies of wood.

Temperate forests are also the sites of some of the major conservation efforts in the world. In the last hundred years, the United States has set aside millions of acres of public land for different purposes, including recreation, wildlife management, and forest resource development. Other countries are following suit, although more slowly.

A strawberry tree frog hides among the plants in a tropical rainforest in Ecuador.

6

TROPICAL RAINFORESTS

Contrary to popular belief, one doesn't always need to swing a machete to clear a path through a tropical rainforest. You might need to hack your way through the tangled edge next to stream beds or along clearings, but once through, the forest opens into a parklike setting, with immensely tall trees shading an open understory. The shade is so deep here that little can grow below the canopy. Tree branches are heavy with many epiphytes—plants that use trees for support but don't parasitize them—and flowers sprout from the base of tree trunks. The canopy is alive with insects, birds, reptiles, and mammals. Eighty percent of the food produced in a tropical forest is in the treetops, so most animals have adopted an arboreal lifestyle to take advantage of this cornucopia.

This fertile environment allows many species to grow much larger than they would in other biomes: 5-foot-wide (1.5-meter-wide) lilypads, 800 foot-long (245-meter-long) lianas (vines), moths with 12-inch (30-cm) wingspans, frogs large enough to eat rats, 60-foot-tall (18-meter-tall) tree ferns, and the largest flowers in the world.

The tropical rainforest is the most diverse and productive biome on the planet. Two and a half acres (1 ha) of forest may contain up to 750 species of tree, 1,500 species of vascular plants, and 42,000 species of insects. This is because the growing conditions are perfect throughout the year. There is plenty of precipitation—between 80 and 300 inches (2 and 8 m) a year—and temperatures are warm, an average of 75 °F (24 °C) year-round. Dry seasons do occur, but they are offset by the rainy seasons and regular precipitation—there are downpours almost every afternoon.

These forests lie between the Tropics of Cancer and Capricorn, 23.5° north and 23.5° south of the equator. Historically, this biologically rich biome covered 9,460,000 square miles (24,500,000 km²) of Earth's land surface, but now, because of conversion to settlement and agriculture, it only covers 3,865,000 square miles (10,000,000 km²), about 7 percent of the land. This amounts to about one-third of the world's total forest-land, but the vegetation is so dense in this biome that tropical forests account for four-fifths of all land plants in the world.

You might assume that since this is such a rich, lush biome, the soils themselves are nutrient-rich. In fact, the opposite is true. Much of the nutrient stock is held in the abundant aboveground vegetation. Very little leaf litter, dead wood, and animal waste remains on the ground for long; it is quickly broken down by termites, bacteria, and fungi. So, although rich, these forests are delicate. If the trees are cut down, what grows in their place is less diverse.

EXPRESSIONS

There are three main expressions of the tropical rainforest biome.

Amazonian

The most extensive tropical forest in the world, the Amazon rainforest covers almost 1.37 billion acres (554 million ha), or 2.7 million square miles

The Amazon River snakes its way through the Amazon rainforest, one of the largest and most biologically rich rainforests in the world.

(7 million km²), including much of the northern half of South America east of the Andes Mountains in Columbia, Ecuador, and Peru. It also extends north into Central America and the Yucatán Peninsula of Mexico, as well as to some of the islands in the Caribbean.

At the heart of the Amazon Hylaea, the South American portion east of the Andes, is the Amazon River. This massive river channels one-sixth of all the fresh water in the world into the Atlantic Ocean, an amount greater than the flow of the next eight largest rivers in the world combined. You can taste its fresh water 100 miles (161 km) out into the ocean.

Many of the plant and animal species here are very rare and endemic, meaning they exist only in this region. The many river and stream channels divide the forest into fragments between which most plants and animals cannot travel. This creates a divided landscape with islands of creatures separated by streams and rivers. Over time, these separate populations evolve different characteristics and become distinct species (this is known as speciation), creating this rarity and endemism.

African

The rainforest of West Africa is the least extensive and the least biologically diverse of all the rainforests. It covers approximately 464 million acres (188 million ha) in Gabon, Congo, and the Central African Republic. Areas of cloud forest, high elevation tropical forest, in Zaire, Rwanda, and Uganda are in danger of disappearing. The Zaire River Basin contains the largest block of rainforest in central Africa.

Although this forest is not much different from the other expressions in structure, the geography is less broken up and restrictive. This allows species to spread more freely, and thus less speciation occurs, resulting in a less diverse grouping of plants and animals than in the other tropical forest regions.

Indo-Malaysian

While the other two expressions straddle the equator, most of the 610 million acres (247 million ha) of Indo-Malaysian tropical rainforests are north of this belt. This includes India, east through Thailand, Cambodia, and Vietnam into the Malaysian archipelago; on Java, New Guinea, the Philippines, and many other islands; as well as in pockets of coastal forest in Queensland, Australia.

The high level of diversity here, while less than in the Amazonian rainforest, is probably the result of the many islands causing speciation over the years. Many animal and plant groups here are similar to those in West Africa, including many bird families.

TROPICAL RAINFOREST PLANTS

Trees of the tropical rainforest biome are usually long-lived organisms. Since the climate is fairly constant all year round, the phenology of rainforest plants is not tied to seasons as it is in the temperate forest. This means that the many different plant species have evolved methods of reproduction to suit their own needs; therefore, flowers and fruit can be found on different trees throughout the year. A single tree may even be going through different stages of leafing, flowering, and fruiting all at once. This prevents the many herbivores from eating all the new growth all at once. The constantly favorable growing conditions also allow most trees to keep their leaves and to photosynthesize year round.

Buttresses, the wide woody flanges at the base of many tropical rainforest trees, are very effective at moving water and nutrients between the roots and leaves. They are also essential for stability since the trees

The Indo-Malaysian rainforests provide homes for many different species than the other rainforest expressions, including tarsiers, a distinct family of primates found only here.

are so shallowly rooted. These roots can quickly take advantage of the abundant rainfall that, with little litter to hold it and release it slowly to tree roots, easily runs off into streams and rivers. Tropical tree roots are also covered with a network of mychorrizae that process the litter into usable nutrients.

There are often three distinct tree layers in tropical forests. The tallest trees—averaging 120 feet (37 m) tall—and as high as 200 feet (61 m)—are known as emergents. They are spaced widely apart and have huge umbrella-like crowns. The crown of a single tree may cover up to an acre of ground. Emergent trees usually have small leaves to help them retain water, otherwise strong winds would dry them out at this height.

The wide spacing of the emergents allows plenty of light through to the next layer. These 80-foot-tall (24-meter-tall) trees form a dense canopy above a more broken, less dense layer of 60-foot-tall (18-meter-tall) trees. The reduced light at this level causes the trees to take on a narrow shape. In addition to the low light, there is little air movement below the canopy, creating high humidity.

Tropical rainforest plants take on many different forms. Trees at lower levels have larger leaves to capture as much sunlight as possible in the low-light conditions.

Beneath these tree layers, the highly shaded shrub layer only receives about 3 percent of the light from above. Many of the shrubs and small trees in this layer are climbers, waiting for a tree to fall so they can shoot up in the new light suddenly afforded by the gap. Palms are common in this layer; this is a very diverse group, with more than 1,000 species in the South American rainforests alone. The ground layer receives even less light, about 1 percent, so there is very little growth there.

Precious Light

Despite the lack of light in the lower layers, some plants have evolved ways of getting enough of this precious resource. The trees below the unbroken canopy tend to have large leaves that can absorb more light than small leaves. Other kinds of plants use the trees themselves for support to get to the light.

Many plants that grow in soil in the temperate forest biome grow as epiphytes—or air plants—here, including orchids, ferns, and cacti. One of the most successful groups of plants in the tropical rainforest, the epiphytes grow in cracks and hollows of tree limbs and trunks; they don't need soil.

Epiphytes don't actually take anything from the tree, like a parasitic fungi would. They just utilize the trees for support. By growing at an elevated level, these plants also benefit from the greater amount of light in the upper levels of the canopy. Occasionally they do harm trees because the sheer weight of so many epiphytes can break limbs. A single tree in South America was found to have more than 2,000 epiphytes growing on it. The smooth bark of many rainforest trees may be an adaptation to discourage these colonist plants from overcrowding.

The stiff leaves of epiphytes trap dust and leaves and, along with the moisture they absorb from the air, process them into nutrients for growth. One group, the bromeliads—the family that includes pineapples—grows abundantly only in the South American rainforests. Their overlapping leaves are very effective at trapping water. These reservoirs are then used by many other arboreal species, including ants and monkeys, for drinking water. Some creatures live only in these oases high in the rainforest canopy. Certain species of epiphytes, the myrmecophytes, have established a special relationship with ants. For example, one of these, the myrmecodia, is not shaped like other epiphytes with their rosettes of leaves to catch debris to turn into food. Instead it has evolved a shape like a potato in order to house ants that provide its food. Inside the myrmecodia are tunnels and chambers that the ants live in. In return for housing, these ants pile their feces in special roots at the center of the plant. This moist, nutrient-rich material nourishes the plants. The ants ensure that they will always have a home by planting the epiphyte's seeds at the base of its host tree.

The myrmecodia's potato-like tuber houses a colony of ants that provide the plant with the nutrients it needs to survive.

Epiphylls are smaller air plants that grow on other plants, such as lichens, algae, and mosses, as well as on animals like crocodiles and turtles. One species even lives on the hair of sloths.

Vines called lianas take advantage of the trees for support, but they do it by climbing. They wind around trees and will even wind around themselves as they climb into any available light-filled gap. They produce flowers at different times than the tree layers they grow into, taking advantage of any available pollinators.

The stranglers, another plant group, use the seeding strategy of epiphytes but then take on the habit of the lianas. Stranglers usually grow from seeds in bird droppings that fall into crevices and hollows on the branches. The developing plants then send roots downward,

Orangutans use lianas to climb into trees for food and to sleep at night.

eventually reaching the soil. The stranglers then grow quickly until they completely surround the host tree, killing it and taking its place. Fig trees are common stranglers in tropical forests.

The largest flower in the world, the *Rafflesia*, also takes advantage of trees, but not for light. *Rafflesia* grow at the base of the trunk, parasitizing the roots for nutrients. One specimen was measured at 38 inches (1 m) and weighed 38 pounds (17 kg). They smell and look like rotten meat in order to attract flies, their main pollinators.

TROPICAL RAINFOREST ANIMALS

As one would expect, the wide diversity of plant life in the tropical rainforest biome supports an equally wide diversity of animals. Most of their activity takes place in the canopy, where most of their food is produced.

Insects in particular occupy the forests here in great numbers and with a wide variety of species. They range in size from tiny hairwing beetles, 0.008 inches (0.02 cm) long, to 13-inch (33 cm) Borneo walking sticks. Beetles and ants are numerous: three square feet (0.9 m^2) of forest may contain eight hundred individual ants of fifty different species.

The sheer numbers of some of these insects are their greatest strength and, in some cases, the reason why they are to be feared and avoided. Army ants in the New World and driver ants in the Old World spend two weeks out of every month marching in huge numbers through the forest, consuming everything in their path. Any unfortunate creature—insect, mammal, bird, even human—will be attacked. Some Indian villages evacuate before the swarm moves through, returning to pest-free homes after the army has passed.

Biting insects are also common; mosquitoes and no-see-ums profit from the humid environment and feast on the blood of the many rainforest creatures. No-see-ums will even drink recently sucked human blood from a mosquito.

Rainforests are quieter than most people expect. The various and numerous plant defenses discourage many herbivores; those that are around are usually secretive and not easy to spot. That said, most rainforest plants are dependent on animals for pollination and seed dispersal. (In the temperate and boreal forests, wind pollination and dispersal play a primary role.)

Flower structure, shape, and scent are usually geared toward a specific pollinator—flowers pollinated by bats open at night, when those creatures are active; bird-pollinated flowers are usually brightly colored

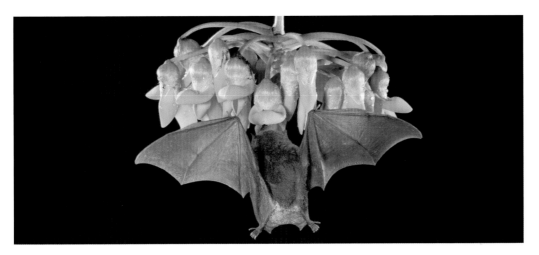

Bats are one of the major pollinators of tropical rainforest plants. This Underwood's long-tongued bat from the cloud forests of Costa Rica is seen here sipping nectar from a cluster of flowers of the mucuna liana.

and scentless, since their pollinators, hummingbirds and sunbirds, are attracted by color and not odor. Seeds are often spread by mammals as well, either by attaching to fur or being swallowed with fruits and expelled along with feces later, usually at a new location.

Animals of the Canopy

Since most of the food in rainforests is in the trees, most animals have evolved efficient ways of getting to it. Many monkeys—including the Asian gibbon, the African colobus monkey, and the Amazonian spider and woolly monkeys—use their prehensile tails as a fifth limb to help them balance on or hang from branches. These agile primates are also able to leap great distances from tree to tree. Although they sometimes do travel to the forest floor, more often than not they stay in the canopy. The diversity of monkeys is greatest in Amazonia; Africa and Indo-Malaysian rainforests each support a great ape species, gorillas and orangutans, respectively. Orangutans spend much of their time in the middle canopy and don't travel very far for food.

Many of the tropical rainforest biome's bird species, like the bird of paradise, the hornbill, and the toucan, are brightly colored and elaborately plumed. This is usually for display purposes but it might also be useful for scaring predators. Another winged creature, the flying fox or giant fruit bat, feeds on fruit and has a wingspan of 5.5 feet (1.7 m).

Many other animals, though not able to fly, have evolved ways to move from tree to tree or from trees to the ground without climbing. Flying lemurs, flying squirrels, flying dragons (lizards, really), flying frogs, and even tree snakes have evolved winglike skin flaps or body shapes that allow them to glide through the canopy.

Predators move silently among the tree branches, hunting the many herbivores in the canopy. At the top of the food chain are the great cats, and the leopard is the greatest of all. The third largest cat in the world, it is feared by all creatures of the South American rainforests. This

A Raggiana Bird of Paradise is one of the many striking birds native to the tropical rainforests of New Guinea.

Although they will climb into trees to rest, ocelots spend most of their time hunting or sleeping on the ground.

and the other great rainforest cats—including the clouded leopard of Southeast Asia, the golden cat of West Africa, and the ocelot of Latin America—prowl both the canopy and the forest floor in their daily hunt for food.

Two of the greatest rainforest predators do not climb to get their prey. The South American harpy eagle and the Philippine eagle are the two largest eagles in the world. They swoop down on their prey— monkeys, sloths, and lemurs—and snatch them quickly out of the trees. Many other aerial predators flourish in this rich environment. The tiny hawk, for example, is very small for a raptor, but it is able to chase and catch hummingbirds and large flying insects.

Animals of the Forest Floor

The creatures of the forest floor forage in the leaf litter. The giant armadillo (in South America) and the pangolin (in Africa) root around for ants, and snakes hunt for bamboo rats and moon rats. Pacas and agoutis (in Central and South America), royal antelope and barking deer (in Africa), and toucans and hornbills forage for the seeds, fruits, flowers, and leaves that rain down from the canopy.

The paca is one of several large rodents in the South American rainforests, feeding on leaves, fruits, and flowers on the forest floor near rivers.

Larger herbivores like Asiatic and African elephants, rhinoceroses, and pygmy hippopotamuses also find plenty of food beneath the rainforest canopy. In Africa, gorillas roam the mountainous cloud forests as well as the lowlands and valleys, feeding on the vegetation and only climbing trees if threatened or to perch for the night.

PEOPLE OF TROPICAL RAINFORESTS

Today there are still some native tribes in tropical rainforests that are not heavily influenced by modern culture. Their way of life is simple and tied directly to their environment. These hunter-gatherer cultures benefit from the year-round availability of food that other forest creatures also depend on. They make everything they need by hand, including clothing and tools. Some tribal people are fairly small and have a low metabolism, which helps them produce less heat and sweat less. (In such a humid environment, sweating is not an effective way to cool the body.) Their wider feet help them to climb trees and cross shallow wetlands more easily.

Many of these cultures are dying out as the world's attention has turned to tropical forests to meet its need for wood. The Indo-Malaysian rainforests are rapidly disappearing as a result of aggressive and wasteful logging practices. Many companies from this region are now cutting Amazon forests quickly for sale to the North American and European markets. Because of the poor soils in this biome, much of this forestland will never grow back, providing no future supplies of wood and eliminating the great biodiversity that may have proved valuable for other reasons, from sources of life-saving drugs to essential food supplies for native peoples and animals.

The Yanomami Amerindians of the Amazon rainforest are one of the largest groups of tribal people who still practice a subsistence lifestyle, farming and hunting, with very little contact from the outside world.

CONCLUSION

FOREST FUTURES

The many problems associated with clear-cutting and other wasteful logging practices are becoming more and more severe as the rainforests and other world forests fall victim to the worldwide demand for wood. Many people take forest products for granted, believing the world has an endless supply. What they don't realize is that the paper towels they use and throw away every day, the pages of a book, or even the logs they burn in a fireplace all come from trees. And since millions of people are using these products, that means millions of trees need to be cut.

Sustainable forestry practices are becoming more popular, although it will be a long time before all major logging companies adopt them. Forest certification programs encourage the use of wood that has been harvested using sustainable methods, like selective cutting that only removes some of the trees and leaves some of the healthier ones as seed sources. One of the best ways people can help to encourage companies to employ these practices is by buying wood and wood products only from suppliers who have this certification. Buying paper that has been made with recycled or non-wood products can help, too.

Forests provide so many benefits to the world and to humans. The best way to ensure that these benefits will continue is to respect and protect this resource. As people learn about the wonders of the forest biome, the more they will see themselves as dependent upon and, more importantly, a part of these natural communities.

GLOSSARY

angiosperm—A plant that reproduces by means of seeds enclosed in fruits; flowering plants; the largest and most diverse division of the plant kingdom.

bromeliad—A family of epiphytic plants of the New World rainforests; members include pineapple and Spanish moss.

cache—An animal's store of food for use in cold or dry times when no other food is available. Squirrels, chipmunks, and blue jays keep caches in trees, burrows, or holes in the ground.

carnivore—An animal that eats mostly meat.

conifer—A gymnosperm; a needle-leaved evergreen tree that reproduces by means of seeds enclosed in cones.

deciduous—Describes trees that drop their leaves at the end of the growing season.

decomposer—An organism, such as a fungus or bacterium, that aids the breakdown of organic material, thereby creating soil.

diapause—A period of time when an organism stops growing temporarily in response to difficult environmental conditions, such as cold or drought.

emergent—Describes a tree that grows well above the canopy trees.

expression—A particular representation of a biome in a given location, for example, the Amazon rainforest is an expression of the tropical rainforest biome in South America.

gymnosperm—A plant that reproduces from "naked" seeds, unlike an angiosperm; these plants include conifers and cycads.

herbivore—An animal that eats mostly plants.

insectivore—An animal that eats mostly insects.

migration—Seasonal movement of animals in response to food and breeding needs.

mutualism—An ecological relationship that is beneficial for both members, such as the one between mychorrizae and trees, or the one between pollinator and plant.

omnivore—An animal that eats all manner of edible material, from meat to plant parts.

parasitism—An ecological relationship that benefits one member at the expense of the other.

pollinator—An animal that, while feeding on nectar, assists a plant in reproducing by unintentionally carrying pollen from a male flower to a female flower.

prehensile—Adapted for seizing, grasping, or holding, like a monkey's tail.

speciation—The process of new species', evolution, usually as the result of isolation of a population from others of the same species due to geographical conditions.

strangler—A plant, usually a liana, that quickly grows to cover its host tree, robbing its resources and killing it.

understory—The lower layer of a forest, including shrubs and saplings. carried out by bacteria, molds, soil invertebrates, and insects.

FIND OUT MORE

Books

Breining, Greg. *The Northern Forest.* New York: Benchmark Books, 2000.

Castner, James. *Surviving in the Rain Forest.* New York: Benchmark Books, 2002.

MacMillan, Dianne M. *Life in a Deciduous Forest.* Minneapolis,
        MN: Lerner Publications Co., 2003.

Web Sites

http://forests.org
Forest Conservation Portal: A conservation based Web site that provides links to many resources about forest ecology, forest conservation, and sites for students.

http://www.cotf.edu/ete/modules/msese/earthsysflr/summary.html
A NASA-sponsored kids earth science Web site with pages on biomes.

http://www.nationalgeographic.com/geographyaction/habitats/forests.html
National Geographic's *Habitats: Home Sweet Home* Web page focusing on forests. Includes "online adventures" in different forests.

http://www.worldlandtrust.org/forestry/
A conservation-focused Web site about forests. Explains why forests are important and shows a case study in conservation.

BIBLIOGRAPHY

Beazley, Mitchell. *The International Book of the Forest.* New York: Simon and Schuster, 1981.

Boreal Forest Network. Winnipeg, Canada, 2002. http://www.borealnet.org/main.html

Cloudsley-Thompson. J. L. *Terrestrial Environments.* London: Croom Helm Ltd., 1975.

Food and Agriculture Organization of the United Nations. *FAO Forestry Paper 140: Global Forest Resources Assessment 2000, Main Report.* Rome: FAO, 2001.

Laurance, William F. "Fragments of the Forest." *Natural History,* July/August, 1998. Marchand, Peter J. *Life in the Cold.* Hanover, NH: University Press of New England, 1996.

Monroe, James S. and Reed Wicander. *Physical Geology: Exploring the Earth, second edition.* Minneapolis/St.Paul: West Publishing Company, 1995.

Packham, J. R., D. J. L. Harding, G. M. Hilton, and R. A. Stuttard. *Functional Ecology of Woodlands and Forests.* London: Chapman and Hall, 1992.

Paulson, Dennis. "Biomes of the World." Tacoma, WA: University of Puget Sound, 1997. http://www.ups.edu/biology/museum/worldbiomes.html

Peterson, Roger Tory. *A Field Guide to the Birds of Eastern and Central North America, fifth edition.* Boston: Houghton Mifflin, Inc., 2002.

Stern, Kingsley R. *Introductory Plant Biology, edition seven.* Dubuque, IA: Wm. C. Brown Publishers, 1997.

Summers, Adam. "Serpents in the Air." *Natural History,* May, 2003.

Warhol, Thomas A. and William A. Patterson III. "Estimating Heat Sums for Remote Location Phenology Sites," unpublished MS research project. University of Massachusetts/Amherst, 1999.

Wilson, Brayton F. *The Growing Tree.* Amherst, MA: The University of Massachusetts Press, 1984.

INDEX

Tom Warhol is a photographer, writer, and naturalist from Massachusetts, where he lives with his wife, their dog, and two cats. Tom holds both a BFA in photography and an MS in forest ecology. Tom has worked for conservation groups such as The Nature Conservancy, managing nature preserves, and The American Chestnut Foundation, helping to grow blight-resistant American chestnut trees. He currently works for the Massachusetts Riverways Program, helping to care for sick, injured, and resident hawks, eagles, and owls. In addition to the Earth's Biomes series, Tom has authored books for Marshall Cavendish Benchmark's AnimalWays series, including *Hawks* and *Eagles.* He also writes for newspapers such as the *Boston Globe.* His landscape, nature, and wildlife photographs can be seen in exhibitions, in publications, and on his Web site, www.tomwarhol.com.